Chroniques de Jane

THE JANE PRINT

KAMELAH BLAIR

Copyright © 2022 Kamelah Blair

Tous les droits sont réservés. Imprimé au Canada.

Aucune partie de ce livre ne peut être utilisée ou reproduite de quelque manière que ce soit sans autorisation écrite, sauf dans le cas de brèves citations incorporées dans des articles critiques ou des critiques

ISBN :978-1-7781160-6-3

enyj Publié par : COJ BOOKZ

DÉDICACE

À mon deux rois. Non seulement tu m'as rendu fier de voir les jeunes hommes que tu es devenus, mais je suis aussi fier de la femme que tu m'as fait devenir. Amour, maman.

CONTENU

Kamelah Blair

1 Plan 1

2 La Fondation 16

3 Développer sans matériel 24

4 L'instabilité avant la chute 42

5 Les ingénieurs 55

6 La sagesse construit une maison 67

7 Fissures Dans La Fondation 73

8 Reconstruire La Fondation 84

9 Le RÉGIME 105

10 L'appel téléphonique 112

KAMELAH BLAIR

Le phénix renaît de ses cendres représente Kamelah Blair. Elle est née et a grandi à Toronto, en Ontario, et a vécu dans la communauté de Jane et Finch. Jane Street était une communauté urbaine soudée composée d'un mélange de familles de la classe moyenne et de la classe supérieure, remplies d'intelligence et d'intelligence de la rue.

Kamelah est PDG de quatre entreprises prospères et mère de deux enfants. Elle est diplômée du George Brown College avec un diplôme spécialisé en administration médicale et technicienne de laboratoire de sang.

La pierre que les bâtisseurs ont refusée était ce qu'elle a utilisé pour construire son empire. Elle est connue comme le mouton noir du côté maternel de la famille et la seule diplômée universitaire du côté paternel de la famille. Son oncle, sa grand-mère, sa marraine, son père et sa belle-mère l'ont encouragée à être meilleure que les choses négatives qu'on lui disait.

CHAPITRE UN :

SCHÉMA DIRECTEUR

Jane n'est pas une personne. Jane est une rue et aussi un mode de vie. En grandissant, Jane n'était qu'un endroit pour moi. Au fil des années, cela a changé. Mais cela signifiait chez moi. Quand je suis sur l'autoroute et que j'entends les bruits de la route, une paix m'envahit, car je sais que je suis proche de Jane et Finch. C'est une bouffée d'air frais. Quand je suis ailleurs, je suis tendu; Je ne sais pas ce que c'est. Jane Street est ma place. C'est chez moi. En vieillissant, j'ai acquis une certaine force et une certaine audace que je crois avoir héritées du fait de vivre au bout de la rue. Quand je suis devenu un peu plus âgé et que j'ai vécu seul, j'ai vécu à Driftwood. Ce sont tous des domaines rivaux, mais j'ai aussi des relations dans ces endroits, alors j'ai traîné des deux côtés de Jane. À mes yeux, Jane est une grande communauté. Je n'y pense pas autrement. A mon époque, c'était juste à la maison. À un moment donné, j'étais très conscient de ne pas aller du côté sud de Jane. Mais que je sois du côté sud ou du côté nord de Jane, la région ne me définit pas. Je suis Jane Street. En fin de compte, c'est ma maison. Jane est l'endroit où j'ai grandi et c'est là que j'ai acquis mon expérience. C'est là que j'ai appris à être moi. Cela

un

impact

sur qui je suis et sur ma façon de voir le monde. Jane est mon encyclopédie personnelle.

Le voyage commence avec mes parents – Yanks mon père et Goldy ma mère – un jeune couple marié vivant dans la rue. Mes deux parents ont grandi en Jamaïque, se sont rencontrés là-bas et sont tombés amoureux là-bas. Ma mère et mon père ont des histoires différentes sur la façon dont ils sont entrés en contact l'un avec l'autre. Ils ont émigré au Canada au début des années 1970 et y ont fondé leur famille. Ma mère m'a mis au monde au mois de septembre. Contrairement à mes parents, je suis né et j'ai grandi dans la région de Jane et Finch. Bien que je sois l'aîné de treize enfants de la famille, j'ai été le seul enfant pendant une longue période. Cependant, je n'étais pas seul. Non seulement j'avais mes parents, mais je considérais aussi certains de mes voisins et mes amis comme ma famille. J'avais ma marraine, Helen, ma tante Pat et mes oncles Jah-Jah et Randy. Nous étions une communauté très soudée. En grandissant, je n'ai pas vécu seul avec mes parents, parce que la vie dans la rue était ce qu'ils vivaient. Au fil du temps, ils se sont séparés, mais ils sont restés légalement mariés. Je ne l'ai jamais compris, mais chacun son truc.

Dans mes premières années, je vivais avec ma mère et mon père. Mon premier souvenir de mes parents étant ensemble, c'est quand Yanks a été arrêté. J'avais entre cinq et sept ans quand j'ai vu mes parents se battre physiquement. Tout a commencé quand ma mère a volé de la drogue à mon père pour la donner à son petit ami. Je savais au fond de moi qu'elle lui était infidèle ; ses actions l'ont montré clairement. Père était venu

maison
consommée

de colère envers elle et, sans hésitation, a confronté ma mère au sujet des médicaments qu'elle avait volés. Je me souviens très bien qu'il portait un pull marron avec des coudes marron foncé et une chemise boutonnée en dessous, et ses mèches étaient coupées bas. Je savais ce que ma mère avait fait, mais je ne voulais rien dire, car j'étais déjà maltraitée physiquement et verbalement par elle, et ils s'étaient disputés avant cet événement à cause de ce que ma mère me faisait. Ma mère, bien sûr, voulait rejeter la faute sur moi, car elle pouvait imaginer la rage que mon père aurait envers elle s'il découvrait la vérité. Eh bien, c'est exactement ce qu'elle a fait – elle m'a épinglé ça. Ma mère était catégorique sur le fait que j'avais pris les médicaments. Cependant, enfant, j'avais une compréhension claire de ce qu'était la drogue et je savais instinctivement que c'était quelque chose de terrible. Je n'y ai donc pas touché. Néanmoins, ma mère a utilisé cette excuse pour faire partir mon père. A l'époque, nous vivions chez Jane et Trethewey. En face de Jane et Trethewey, il y avait un immeuble Metro Housing d'environ cinq étages. Il y avait un long couloir assez grand pour accueillir plusieurs unités. Mlle Rose, qui était ma baby-sitter et brigadier scolaire à l'époque, habitait au deuxième étage, au même étage que mes parents. Cependant, nous vivions aux extrémités opposées du long couloir. Je passais la plupart de mon temps chez elle, parce que je voulais échapper à ma mère. La violence physique et verbale n'a pas été bénéfique pour ma croissance et mon développement mental. Vous devez réellement être dans une situation comme la mienne, ou similaire, pour savoir ce que j'articule. Ann, l'amie de ma mère, vivait au premier étage, et le meilleur ami de mon père, Jermaine, et sa petite amie, Diana, vivaient au quatrième étage. Diana était une

qui
,

belle dame de 5 pieds 5 pouces avec une peau claire, et Jermaine était un homme grand, musclé et à la peau foncée qui prenait beaucoup de drogues illicites, y compris des médicaments pour les hauts et les basaffecté ses émotions et ses sautes d'humeur.

Un jour, j'ai désobéi à ma mère, parce qu'elle voulait que je reste à l'intérieur, mais je ne voulais pas faire ça. J'avais demandé à jouer chez Jermaine et Diana, car ils avaient aussi de jeunes enfants et ils étaient mes camarades de jeu, mais Goldy a dit "Non". J'ai décidé d'utiliser la psychologie inversée et je lui ai demandé si je pouvais aller chez Miss Rose. Je portais une robe bleu bébé à pois et une touche de rouge au col, et mes cheveux étaient en nattes. Dès qu'elle a dit "oui", j'ai couru dans le couloir, et alors que je courais dans le couloir, j'ai regardé en arrière et elle était là, ma mère, jetant un coup d'œil pour s'assurer que j'allais à l'appartement de ma baby-sitter. Quand j'ai entendu la porte se refermer, j'ai pris l'escalier et je suis allé chez mes amis. J'ai apporté des jouets avec moi, dont des poupées Barbie et Jem et les hologrammes. Quand je suis entré chez Jermaine et Diana, Diana était toujours avec des béquilles suite à une altercation qu'elle avait eue quelques semaines auparavant. Je n'ai pas été témoin de la dispute entre eux; cependant, j'avais entendu les mères du quartier en parler, et mon amie et moi avions aussi eu une petite discussion sur ce qui s'était passé.

Soudain, pendant que nous jouions, Jermaine est rentré bouleversé et est allé dans la cuisine pour prendre une bière. Lui et Diana ont commencé à se disputer, et il a sorti un couperet sur elle. Je l'ai entendu dire : "Si tu n'arrêtes pas de mentir,

, je vais te couper la main." Finalement, il lui a coupé la main sur la porte du congélateur et elle est entrée dans le salon avec sa main enveloppée dans une serviette en papier marron. J'étais pétrifié et je lui ai dit que je rentrais chez moi. Il a dit: "Non, tu ne peux pas." J'ai répondu immédiatement : "Mais je ne vis pas ici !" Jermaine n'agissait pas du tout comme un homme normal. Il n'a clairement pas aimé ma réponse; Je l'ai vu dans son expression faciale. Il était furieux au point où il a mis Diana, les enfants et moi dans leur chambre, a verrouillé la porte, puis est sorti dans le salon sans exprimer de remords. Les enfants se sont mis à pleurer. Leurs pleurs m'ont révélé que c'était un de ses comportements habituels. Ils avaient l'habitude de les voir se battre, mais vous auriez pu voir que cet exemple de relation entre un homme et une femme était loin d'être accepté. Quinze minutes se sont écoulées et Jermaine est revenu dans la pièce et nous a demandé si nous voulions une collation. J'ai refusé et lui ai dit que je voulais juste rentrer chez moi. Il a dit : "Désolé, Tiny, je ne peux pas faire ça." Tiny est un surnom que j'avais étant enfant. En disant cela, il n'avait pas l'air contrarié ; au lieu de cela, il avait un comportement agréable. Néanmoins, cela ne l'a pas empêché de nous enfermer tous les quatre dans le placard. À ce moment-là, je me suis dit : *"J'aurais dû écouter ma mère et rester à la maison."* Être dans le placard n'était pas la meilleure sensation. Le placard était sombre et j'étais mort de peur. Les paroles de ma mère se répétaient dans ma tête. J'aurais certainement dû l'écouter.

Nous étions tous là-dedans pendant un temps exceptionnellement long, puis il est venu nous chercher. Il nous a ensuite mis dans le placard de leur chambre. Les meubles de la chambre étaient tout en bois et c'était cher à l'époque. J'ai vu que ils avaient une petite télévision, et elle était au-dessus de la commode. Alors que j'observais leur chambre, Jermaine nous a transférés dans la pièce voisine, puis il s'est dirigé vers les toilettes. Pendant qu'il était dans les toilettes, nous avons trouvé une stratégie d'évasion, avons rapidement saisi le moment et nous nous sommes enfuis. C'était en fait comme si nous avions échappé à un enlèvement. Cela n'avait aucun sens d'aller au deuxième étage où j'habitais, alors à la place, nous sommes allés au premier étage où habitait Ann. Au moment où nous sommes arrivés au premier étage, nous pouvions l'entendre descendre les marches.

Nous avions tellement peur que nous nous sommes cachés au bas des marches où se trouvait la zone de stockage. Ann jouait de la musique forte; par conséquent, elle ne nous a pas entendus crier, et les immeubles de Metro Housing avaient des murs minces et n'étaient pas construits de la meilleure façon. Il nous a finalement trouvés et nous avons dû retourner dans leur unité. En passant devant la porte de Miss Rose, nous avons crié et hurlé, mais elle ne pouvait pas non plus nous comprendre. Je n'étais pas sûr de ce qu'elle faisait ce jour-là. Nous étions de nouveau kidnappés. J'utilise le mot kidnappé pour décrire ses actions parce que, pour moi, c'était ce que ça ressemblait. Il nous a remis dans leur chambre pendant encore quinze minutes et a verrouillé la porte. Pendant ce temps, l'eau tombait du corps de Jermaine et Diana avait une fontaine qui coulait de ses yeux. Ils semblaient tous les deux avoir peur, mais la peur de Jermaine était un autre type de peur, celle où vous feriez n'importe quoi, et cela inclut de commettre un meurtre. Étant présente dans une atmosphère comme la leur, tout ce que je voulais dire c'était : "Tu peux garder mes jouets. Tout ce que je veux, c'est rentrer chez moi. Nous sommes passés devant chez moi en venant ici." Mais les mots ne sont jamais sortis de ma bouche, même si je les ai répétés encore et encore dans ma tête.

6
Chronicles of Jane: The Jane Print

Son comportement a commencé à changer et il a commencé à appeler Diana des noms dégradants, comme "salope" et "pute". Il a également mentionné ma mère de cette manière. Ils ont fait des allers-retours pendant environ une heure. Il lui a alors dit : « Toi, Goldy, et tes autres amis dites du mal de moi ! Qu'as-tu à me dire maintenant ? Vous ne nettoyez pas la maison et vous ne faites rien ! Jermaine et Diana ont continué à se disputer. Soudain, il la poussa contre la commode. Et puis il lui a demandé : "Est-ce que tu vas me dire la vérité ?"

Elle a répondu: "Je ne sais pas de quoi tu parles. Que veux-tu me dire maintenant?"

Il s'est alors tourné vers nous, les enfants qu'il retenait captifs. Nous étions debout, emmitouflés de peur de l'autre côté de la pièce. Il nous a regardés droit dans les yeux et a dit : "Voilà ce qui se passe quand vous êtes avec un homme et que vous dites-lui un mensonge. Il a sorti un pistolet de la taille de son pantalon, a pointé le bout du pistolet sur sa tête et a appuyé sur la gâchette. Juste comme ça, il l'a tuée d'un coup, à travers la télé. Le temps s'est figé. J'étais sans voix. Quand je suis revenue à la réalité, j'ai immédiatement pris conscience que les enfants pleuraient et j'ai commencé à les consoler, oui, dans mon état dévasté. Cette situation m'avait causé de la douleur, mais elle m'avait aussi appris à prendre soin des autres. en un instant, tout ce que j'avais en moi était un câlin. Je n'avais littéralement aucun mot de réconfort.

Je les serrais si fort qu'il n'y avait pas d'espace pour que l'air puisse passer. Leur monde venait de s'effondrer juste devant eux. Je n'étais pas un enfant gros, je n'étais pas non plus, maigre mais nos os se sont connectés si rapidement. Nous avions vraiment besoin de réconfort l'un de l'autre. La douleur a inondé nos jeunes âmes. C'était une expérience traumatisante que j'allais ne souhaite absolument personne.

Je ne sais pas quand Jermaine a quitté l'appartement, mais il est allé au deuxième étage, où nous vivions. Ma mère, qui était enceinte à l'époque, lui a ouvert la porte de son plein gré, ne sachant pas ce qui se passait. Il était le bienvenu chez nous à tout moment. Elle a quitté sa présence pour aller aux toilettes et il a décidé de lui tirer dessus. Elle est tombée à côté de son lit à baldaquin et est allée en dessous. Et elle y est restée.

Ma mère a dit que la seule raison pour laquelle elle lui avait ouvert la porte était qu'il était le meilleur ami de mon père. Il est allé à l'étage de l'autre dame et a commencé à lui tirer dessus. Je ne sais pas si elle a reçu une balle dans la jambe ou la cheville. Puis il est allé au premier étage, où habitait Ann, le même appartement où nous avons essayé d'aller la première fois. Il a fini par lui tirer une balle dans l'épaule. Il revenait à l'étage, et le bâtiment était dans un chahut complet, alors que les gens frappaient à la porte. J'étais encore dans mon état figé. Peu de temps après tout cela, il s'est suicidé. Après, je n'ai pas parlé pendant un an. Non seulement j'étais muet, mais j'ai aussi commencé à devenir somnambule. Et dire que tout cela était dû aux problèmes de drogue du meilleur ami de mon père.

En 1985, après l'incident, mon frère est né. Peu de temps après, j'ai été envoyé en Jamaïque pour des vacances, car je ne parlais pas.

Pendant que j'y étais, j'ai toujours eu des flashbacks de ce que j'aurais pu faire différemment. J'ai perdu le contact avec les filles de Diana, mais elles m'ont toujours manqué en tant qu'amies et j'ai souvent pensé à elles, puisque nous avons tous été témoins de l'incident qui s'est produit dans notre communauté. Je me suis toujours demandé ce qu'ils ressentaient en sachant que c'était leur mère qui était décédée sous leurs yeux. J'ai dit à mon père, en 2019, que je lui en voulais, mais j'aime tellement mon père. Je lui en voulais parce que c'était son meilleur ami, et il n'a rien fait. Mon père m'a dit : « Je n'aurais rien pu faire par rapport à la situation, car il s'est suicidé. S'il ne s'était pas suicidé, bien sûr, j'aurais fait quelque chose. Quand le meilleur ami de mon père a coupé la main de sa petite mère, j'aurais dû observer ce qui se passait, mais encore une fois, j'étais un enfant et je ne croyais pas aux histoires d'adultes dont parlaient ma mère et ses amis, qui inclus des histoires sur mon père. J'ai balayé ce que ma mère et ses amis faisaient. En tant qu'enfant, cela ne m'a jamais incité à m'impliquer dans la conversation des adultes. C'est alors que j'ai appris, encore aujourd'hui, à observer minutieusement chaque situation. J'ai tendance à trop réfléchir et j'observe chaque situation du début à la fin. Cette situation m'a amené à commencer à me comporter de cette manière. Nous avons continué à vivre dans ce même complexe d'appartements pendant une courte période, puis je suis finalement allé vivre à Malton avec ma marraine, Helen. Malton était un quartier chic, comme Richmond Hill, à l'époque.

J'ai eu le meilleur des deux mondes. J'ai eu le privilège de vivre une vie de ghetto - la drogue, le meurtre, les disputes et l'argent rapide

Fresh -

et j'ai aussi pu vivre une vie comme *Prince of Bel-Air* -un vie de grande classe. Helen était une femme jamaïcaine de principes et de normes. Elle était infirmière et entrepreneure. Elle mesurait cinq pieds cinq pouces, avait une chevelure pleine et une voix douce. Elle était craignant Dieu, aimante, attentionnée et ambitieuse. Quand j'avais des ennuis, son style de discipline consistait à me faire repasser tout le linge et à éplucher un sac de pommes de terre. Après avoir fini ma punition, elle m'asseyait alors dans la deuxième salle familiale. Elle expliquait mes actions et la raison de ma punition, puis elle me demandait : « Que feriez-vous différemment ? Cette question m'a permis de réfléchir à mes actions. Ses compétences disciplinaires ont contribué à faire de moi la femme que je deviens aujourd'hui.

Helen était une femme heureuse, et cela se manifestait tout le temps chez elle. Elle m'a occupé avec du ballet, des claquettes, du jazz et de la gymnastique. Nous avions un chien nommé Harlem et deux oiseaux. L'un des oiseaux était vert et jaune, et l'autre était bleu et jaune. Ma vie était plus structurée et je n'ai subi aucun traumatisme. Dans la maison d'Helen, il y avait une

horloge grand-père de huit pieds, et au bas de l'horloge se trouvait un espace de rangement. À ce moment tragique, je pouvais me cacher dans la partie inférieure de cette horloge ou m'asseoir devant et regarder le temps passer. Elle m'a permis de le faire et n'a jamais posé de questions. Elle m'apportait parfois ma couverture ou me demandait si je voulais une collation. C'était une évasion pour moi chaque fois que j'allais chez ma marraine. Nous avons mangé autour de la table ensemble, cuisiné ensemble et cuisiné ensemble. C'était plus comme *le décor du Cosby Show* . J'ai appris l'amour et je l'ai ressenti d'elle. Ma mère, sur les

, ne m'a jamais montré ce type d'amour. C'était comme si je n'étais pas important pour elle. Mon père m'a montré et m'a appris l'amour, et il m'a prêché quotidiennement, malgré son style de vie. Cependant, quand j'étais avec mon père, je n'étais jamais à l'aise, car je devais toujours regarder par-dessus mon épaule.

Un jour fidèle, avant de vivre avec Helen, la police est venue chercher mon père. Il portait un pantalon bleu, rouge et gris et une chemise grise. Son maillot de corps était visible et, à ce moment-là, il avait commencé à faire repousser ses dreadlocks. Il m'a jeté sur son dos, à la manière d'un ferroutage, et il a pris six volées d'escaliers. Quand nous sommes arrivés au sixième étage, la police cherchait un homme qui correspondait à la description de mon père. Ils ont dit son nom au gouvernement ainsi que ses pseudonymes sur les talkies-walkies. Mon père a commencé à frapper à des portes au hasard. Je n'oublierai jamais qu'une petite dame est sortie, et il lui a demandé, tout en retirant de l'argent, "Pouvez-vous juste la regarder pendant une heure?" Au début, elle a eu l'air surprise, puis elle a juste dit : "D'accord".

La police montait au troisième étage. J'y suis resté environ trois ou quatre heures, mais la dame ne mangeait pas de sucre, donc elle ne pouvait pas m'offrir de sucreries. Et elle ne regardait pas la télé, alors nous nous sommes juste assis et avons écouté la radio. Les dernières nouvelles sont tombées et j'ai entendu le nom de mon père. Elle m'a regardé, mais je n'ai jamais levé les yeux; J'ai juste fait comme si je ne connaissais pas le nom. Ils ont dit quelque chose comme un incident qui s'est produit dans cette zone, mais je n'ai pas réagi. Encore une fois, je n'ai rien dit, parce que c'était la voie de la rue. Puis j'ai entendu quelqu'un frapper à la porte,

et c'était l'un des amis de mon père. J'ai couru vers lui et elle a tout de suite compris que je le connaissais. Il a dit "Merci" et il lui a offert plus d'argent.

Elle dit calmement : « Non, le monsieur m'avait déjà donné de l'argent. "Non, prends-le. C'est bon. Nous apprécions que tu l'aies regardée pendant plus d'une heure."

Elle s'est tournée vers lui à la porte et lui a demandé si tout allait bien, et s'il voulait que je reste là plus longtemps. Je ne l'ai pas regardée, mais j'ai souri.

"Non, ça va. Elle va bien, mais merci », a dit gentiment l'ami de mon père. Il m'a ramené chez ma mère, et je n'ai pas revu mon père pendant un moment. Il ne serait pas présent dans ma vie pendant trois semaines, puis c'est revenu à normal après. Cela arrivait souvent. J'allais à l'école dans le coin, et après l'école, on s'arrêtait aux immeubles. Mon père m'amenait acheter un goûter, et je n'hésitais pas à prendre mes deux dollars pour acheter des frites et sauce. Deux dollars étaient sous forme de facture papier à l'époque. Après avoir quitté le magasin, nous traversions généralement la rue pour rentrer à la maison. J'aimais faire cela quand j'étais enfant. Quand tout cela était fait, je prenais mon prendre un bain, manger mon dîner et lire quelques livres avant d'aller au lit. Le bruit fréquent des coups de feu sur Jane Street m'a déclenché. Je sentais instantanément de l'eau couler de moi et je ressentais le besoin de me cacher. Oui, la transpiration est un signeof

Jane: The Jane Print

Après que le somnambulisme ait continué, ma mère a compris que quelque chose n'allait pas avec moi, parce que je ne pouvais pas Je ne me souviens même pas que j'avais fait du somnambulisme la nuit précédente. Pendant mon somnambulisme, j'ouvrais la porte et je finissais par retourner dans l'appartement de mon ami. Puis un jour, j'ai fini par sortir et quelqu'un m'a ramené dans le hall. Ma mère me cherchait déjà et elle m'a battu en plus. Cela s'est passé pendant six à huit mois après l'incident de la fusillade. Plus tard, je suis retourné vivre avec Helen, qui m'a élevé à plein temps. Cependant, je rendais visite à ma mère le week-end. Le somnambulisme s'est arrêté et je n'en ai plus jamais ressenti en vivant avec ma marraine pendant un an.

Finalement, Helen a décidé qu'elle déménageait à Newmarket, qui était un tout nouvel endroit à l'époque. Je me souviens que le jardin n'avait que de la boue et de la terre. Elle était en transition et je savais que je ne serais pas là avant longtemps. En temps voulu, je suis retourné à Jane Street pour vivre avec ma mère. Le somnambulisme a recommencé, tout comme les crimes quotidiens dont j'ai été témoin. Après être retourné à Jane Street, je suis allé en Jamaïque pendant un certain temps. Ma mère avait son propre traumatisme à surmonter, alors elle a déménagé dans la maison de sa mère sur Jane Street et Grandravine Drive (Down the Lane).

Je suis allé dans un collège catholique pendant un certain temps. Je venais de rentrer de la Jamaïque, alors, bien sûr, j'avais un accent et je parlais vite. Et, croyez-le ou non, quand j'étais plus jeune, je bégayais. L'école m'a envoyé en thérapie pour corriger mon problème de bégaiement. Le milieu catholique

m'a
expulsé

parce que, le mercredi des Cendres, j'ai refusé de laisser le prédicateur saisir mon visage et mettre des cendres sur mon front. L'altercation du mercredi des Cendres m'a conduit au bureau. La semaine suivante, c'était la communion. Ils m'ont associé à un autre étudiant nommé Patrick. Il avait un passé jamaïcain, donc il me comprenait mieux. Ils voulaient que je m'assoie dans une boîte et que je raconte mes problèmes à un parfait inconnu, mais j'ai refusé. Ils m'ont forcé à le faire, parce que c'était la règle. Quand je suis finalement entré dans la boîte, après avoir désobéi, le prédicateur a dit quelques Je vous salue Marie, et il a demandé : « À quand remonte votre dernière confession ?

J'ai dit : « Je ne me confesse pas à l'humanité. Si j'ai un problème, je parle à Dieu, mon Père ou mon père charnel.

Il secoua la porte et répéta la question : « Quelle est votre confession ?

J'ai dit : « Je ne te raconte pas mes putains de problèmes. Qui es-tu pour me dire quoi que ce soit ? Tu n'es pas mon Dieu Père, et tu n'es pas mon père charnel.

Le prêtre se leva brusquement et sortit en trombe de la boîte. Il m'a attrapé le bras et m'a secoué. J'ai dit non. Qui es-tu? Ne me touche pas ! Cela a mené à mon expulsion de toutes les écoles catholiques de Toronto.

Ma mère et ma tante sont venues à l'école et ont dit: «Eh bien, vous auriez dû nous expliquer quand nous nous sommes inscrits ici que ces choses se produiraient, car elle vient des Caraïbes et elle ne Je ne sais pas ces choses. Tu aurais dû lui expliquer, au lieu de la forcer ! Je m'en foutais vraiment à ce moment-là, je voulais juste le combattre pour avoir mis la main sur moi.

CHAPITRE DEUX :

LA FONDATION

Ma grand-mère maternelle, Gloria, et ma marraine, Helen, étaient les meilleures amies. Helen est la façon dont Gloria est venue au Canada. Je me souviens qu'Helen a offert de l'argent à Gloria pour me garder, mais Gloria a refusé. Je ne savais pas pourquoi elle refuserait à sa propre petite-fille de venir habiter chez elle. Mais j'en ai conclu qu'elle ne voulait tout simplement pas de moi chez elle. Lorsque je suis revenu de la Jamaïque au Canada, je suis allé vivre avec ma mère et ma grand-mère dans la région de Jane et Grandravine. Je connaissais déjà beaucoup de gens au sein de cette communauté. C'était à cause de la traction de mon père. Mon père et moi avions l'habitude de voyager ensemble souvent, donc je connaissais beaucoup d'endroits et beaucoup de gens. Jane et Grandravine avaient deux parties : Bottom Lane et Top Lane. Nous vivions sur Bottom Lane. Je jouais toute la journée, sachant que mon père était dans le coin, cela m'a rassuré. J'avais quelques baby-sitters qui s'occupaient de moi dans ce quartier, et j'étais plus présente chez elles que chez ma grand-mère. Parfois, je finissais par dormir chez eux.

16
Chroniques de Jane : L'estampe de Jane

Une fois de plus, j'avais appris à être une personne observatrice, alors quand ma grand-mère a exprimé ses sentiments au sujet de ma vie avec elle à Helen, j'ai su qu'il y avait un problème. J'ai essayé de rester hors de son chemin autant que possible. Helen n'était pas tout le temps à la maison, à cause du type de travail qu'elle faisait, et elle n'aimait pas que je sois seule à la maison. Elle avait six enfants à elle, mais j'étais le plus jeune. Gloria et Helen ne se sont jamais disputées, mais un jour, elles ont eu une vive discussion à mon sujet. Je suis juste passé devant eux et je suis allé jouer. Dans la maison de ma grand-mère, il y avait moi, ma tante Pat et mon oncle Benkey. Mon oncle Mark passait régulièrement. J'étais toujours à l'intérieur et à l'extérieur de la maison, parce que je ne me sentais pas à l'aise d'être là. Cependant, mon père apportait de l'argent pour ma mère et moi, ou il achetait des produits d'épicerie pour la famille.

Un jour d'automne, qui correspondait à la rentrée des classes, Gloria préparait le dîner du dimanche. Je suis entré et j'ai dit "soir" à tout le monde, et elle m'a dit "non, vous devriez nous appeler par notre nom". J'étais confus, mais je savais qu'elle avait de la famille aux États-Unis. Sa sœur, ma tante Pat, a dit à haute voix : « Mais elle nous a déjà salués. Il n'a pas besoin d'être ainsi. J'ai posé mes affaires, puis je suis parti. Quand je suis revenu, j'avais faim. À l'époque, ma cousine, Pula, vivait avec nous. C'était une enfant potelée. Elle était très intelligente mais pas intelligente du tout, car elle était hébergée par ses parents et notre grand-mère. Elle était très gâtée et très appréciée de la famille. Gloria m'a dit que je devais attendre qu'elle ait fini de manger pour manger. Je n'ai pas eu de problème avec ça, mais je me demandais pourquoi. Parfois, j'attendais, mais je finissais

par
m'endormir

. Pendant la nuit, mon oncle faisait des macaronis au fromage et des hot-dogs. Je me suis réveillé en le faisant, et il m'en a donné. Cela a continué à se produire, mais ma mère n'était pas au courant que cela se passait. Cependant, je n'allais rien dire. Un jour, ma grand-mère m'a dit : « Si tu as faim, alors quand ta cousine aura fini de manger, tu devrais manger dans son assiette. J'ai immédiatement réagi en disant: "Mon père paie pour tout ce qui est cuisiné dans cette maison." J'ai ensuite claqué la porte et elle a ouvert la fenêtre pour avouer quel était son problème avec moi. Elle m'a ensuite avoué quel était son problème avec moi. J'ai découvert qu'elle ne me détestait pas mais plutôt mon père. Ma grand-mère pensait que mon père avait drogué son fils Jah-Jah, mais ce n'était pas le cas. Alors qu'elle pleurait, elle a avoué qu'elle ne m'aimait pas à cause de ce que mon père avait fait.

J'ai fièrement défendu mon père. Je savais qu'il ne ferait jamais quelque chose comme ça, à cause des nombreuses conversations que nous avions eues. Il parlerait aussi à mon oncle. J'ai dit à ma grand-mère qu'elle s'était trompée dans son histoire et elle était furieuse. Elle voulait que je quitte définitivement sa maison. Elle n'aimait pas l'idée que je lui réponde, alors j'ai quitté la maison. J'ai revu mon père quelques heures plus tard et je lui ai raconté tout ce qui se passait dans la maison. Il était furieux. Il a affirmé qu'il donnait de l'argent à ma famille et achetait des produits d'épicerie pour la maison. Ma mère avait déménagé avant cet incident et vivait avec son petit père, alors quand il est venu aider à faire face à la situation, ma mère est finalement venue aussi, et il lui a dit qu'elle avait besoin d'avoir un logement à elle. Tante Pat

18
Chroniques de Jane : The Jane Print

est intervenue et a dit que je pouvais rester dans sa chambre. Tout le monde était d'accord, mais je n'avais pas le droit de quitter la pièce. Je devais rester dans la chambre à tout moment. Oncle Randy était un bon basketteur et il revenait des États-Unis au moment où tout le drame se produisait. Je savais déjà qu'il avait été envoyé chez sa mère, d'après ce que son père lui avait dit aux États-Unis, mais je n'ai jamais rien dit, parce que ce n'était pas ma place. Helen était dans sa nouvelle maison, et elle y était depuis trois mois. Ils étaient encore en train de construire la maison. Je me souviens d'avoir visité le nouvel endroit, mais rien n'a été fait, pas même l'arrière-cour ou la cuisine. Encore une fois, Helen ne voulait pas que je sois là, car j'étais la plus jeune et j'avais tendance à toucher à tout. J'étais chez ma grand-mère pendant environ trois ou quatre mois. Je me souviens d'être rentré à la maison un soir, et de nulle part, mon oncle m'a dit : « J'ai entendu ce qui se passe. je vous dis juste; ce n'était pas ton père qui prenait la drogue. Et ton père m'a dit pourquoi il avait rompu avec ta mère. Des choses arrivent. Je ne veux pas que tu sois comme ton père.

Oncle Jah-Jah et moi partageons le même anniversaire. Il m'a offert une poupée Cabbage Patch. Le lendemain matin, je ne sais pas si Gloria nous avait entendu parler, mais je suis rentré de l'école et je n'ai pas trouvé ma poupée Cabbage Patch. Mon oncle a acheté plus d'articles pour ma poupée et a proposé de m'en acheter un nouveau. Il m'a dit que ça allait. Nous nous sommes juste assis là et nous nous sommes souri jusqu'à ce que je m'endorme. Pula, mon cousin, a admis que ma grand-mère l'avait jeté, et mon oncle et moi sommes allés à la poubelle pour le chercher. Mon oncle a fini par acheter de nouveaux articles pour ma poupée. J'ai passé beaucoup de temps avec ma baby-sitter et ses enfants. Elle était

gentille
si

. Tout le monde connaissait mon père; par conséquent, je n'ai jamais eu faim.

Finalement, j'ai vécu avec Helen dans sa nouvelle maison, puis je suis allé chez ma mère. Ma mère avait trouvé sa place chez son nouveau gentleman, Charles. À cette époque, elle avait déménagé à Rexdale, Jamestown. Je vivais à plein temps avec ma mère, mais je rendais visite à mon père ou à Helen le week-end. Mon père avait des rivaux à Jamestown, alors il préférait que je le rencontre à mi-chemin chaque fois qu'il venait me chercher. Il vivait à Falstaff. Le dimanche, j'allais à l'église du palais de prière. J'avais l'habitude de sauter l'église, parce que je voulais passer du temps avec mon père. Je prenais le bus de l'école du dimanche pour me rendre à l'église, puis j'abandonnais pour rendre visite à mon père. J'allais à l'église avec mon petit frère, alors je l'ai payé en bonbons et deux dollars pour qu'il se taise. J'ai toujours essayé de me précipiter et de revenir à temps. Bien sûr, il y a eu un dimanche où j'ai raté le bus scolaire, et le pasteur a dû me ramener à la maison, et, oui, ma mère m'a battu le cul. She was more upset that I had taken my brother out of church and on the journey to see my father. After getting busted, I wasn't allowed to see my father from that time onward. My brother just couldn't keep quiet. By this time, the abuse had increased. I don't know why my mother was so angry with me. Even when I did nothing wrong, I would get the short end of the stick. I don't know what it was.

My mother was pregnant with her fourth child, for her current partner, and they held a lot of parties. My house was the party house back then.

One day, Goldy went grocery shopping, so I took it upon myself to go downstairs, turn on the big sound system, and put on a few records. I turned the music up and scratched away, having the time of my life. Music has always been an outlet for me to escape pain or past traumatic thoughts that crossed my mind. I did not know that my mother was watching me from outside, through the basement window. When she came into the house, she called me and asked me if I had touched the sound system. I lied to her and said, "No. I was playing with my Walkman." I then told her the truth, and I let her know why I touched the sound system and even went into detail as to why I picked the songs I was playing. One of the songs I played was "Can't Touch This" by MC Hammer. I was a part of the upcoming talent show at school. I knew what was coming. My mom brought me to the basement steps and kicked me down the stairs three times. Then she locked the door, and I had to stay down there. I didn't mind, because at least I could be locked off from the world upstairs. The basement was fully furnished, and we had a TV and a fluffy rug. Charles would try to intervene and tell her that she shouldn't be doing this to me. He knew my father and the power that he had. He explained to her that he didn't want to witness the abuse that was occurring. Furthermore, he didn't want me to tell my dad. He would try to save me, but I knew Friday was coming, and I didn't care. Friday was the day for me to escape to my father's place for the weekend.

At that same time, Jamestown had two courts. It was the place that my cousins and I played tag. Classic Burger King was the place to hang

out, and Don and I would play outside often. One Wednesday afternoon after middle school, we played. She was at the top of the court, and I was at the other end of the court. While we were playing tag, the game suddenly turned into a water fight. I was soaking wet, and I had a curfew. I had to be home by five o'clock, but that wasn't the case that afternoon. My mom was working nights at the time. She was an intelligent woman but also weird. She was two different women in front of different people. While at work, she talked and carried herself in a different way. When she was around her friends, the Kingstonians, the gangster would kick in. My mother was definitely a smoker, and on Sunday evenings, she would prepare her weed religiously. She would then put them in her flat metallic cigarette case. When I noticed it was six o'clock, I ignored the time and continued to play. Romping was my thing, and I didn't want to leave. Time flew by, and soon it was nine o'clock and people were going home. I decided to go to my cousin's house, because I didn't want to face my mom. I knew what was going to happen. As soon as I got to my cousin's house, her mom looked at me and said, "Your mother is looking for you." My house was two minutes away from the courts, but it took me an hour to get there, because I was pacing. I wanted to get dry, because I didn't want my mom to see me soaking wet. Unfortunately, my pacing didn't work. When I got to the house, she was already at the door, waiting for me. I was focused on going up the steps. Funny enough, my mom didn't beat me that night, but the following morning I was awakened by a whole glass of water. She said, "You want to be wet? Here's wet." She grounded me, and I wasn't allowed outside. After some time, she

wanted me to leave the house, but only to go to the store to get batteries for the TV remote. We had a remote control that could be pushed into the TV, and, of course, she thought I had lost it. But it was Jesus, my brother, who had lost it. Nevertheless, I got the blame for it. So, with my smart mouth I said, "Well, but I thought I wasn't allowed outside." I even had a smirk on my face; I was twelve years old at this point. This really upset her. She told me that I was rebellious, and I told her that she was being ridiculous. Later on, she sent me away to my father's place. My mother didn't discipline me; she abused me. I stopped attending school, and at the age of thirteen, I ceased living with my mother. Whenever my mother would beat me, she would say that I had told my father about the drugs. At first, I didn't understand what she was saying to me. I would freeze every time she mentioned the drugs. Then I started to recall what happened in the past. She was angry with her life, and she was never stable again.

CHAPTER THREE:

DEVELOPING WITHOUT MATERIALS

When I lived in Jamaica as a child, my aunt would send me different things from the States, including clothes, shoes, and even snacks. At one point, she sent me a five-pack of Hubba Bubba gum, and each pack of pink gum held five or six pieces. One day, I gave a young boy named Dwayne some of my gum. A week went by, and I noticed that he was still chewing the exact same piece of gum, so I asked him, "Dwayne, how are you still chewing the gum 'til now?" He explained that he thought that was the only piece left, so he tried to preserve it for as long as possible. When I told him I had more, he started to fight with me, asking why I didn't tell him and give him more. It turned out to be a big fight, and he was so upset that he found a stone near my house, and he threw it at me and hit my head. I was tempted to fight him, but I thought at that moment, *"I don't know how to fight a Jamaican!"* When I got home, my aunt was enraged, and she asked what happened. I wasn't trained to lie, but I knew how to twist a story. So, I told her a

story about Dwayne and I playing and accidentally getting hurt. A week or so later, I saw Dwayne and the other kids on the road. I invited them to play Duck-Duck-Goose, a popular Canadian game. Usually, I would go outside barefoot, since that was something the Jamaican kids did regularly, although it would piss my aunt off when I would leave the house that way. She didn't want me to conform to some of the kids' ways of doing things, but rather hold true to my Canadian upbringing. But at that time, I didn't care, because on that specific day, I had a plan. I wore my nicest Nike's, and I invited the kids to sit down and play. I then initiated a game of Duck-Duck-Goose. Since it was still quite a new game for everyone, they immediately ran to play with me. When it was my turn, I made sure that when I stood up, I dusted off myself. I was wearing peach shorts and a peach and blue top. As I went around the circle, I gave Dwayne a big slap on his head, and I yelled out, "Goose!" I took off running and never stopped. He was running close behind me, but I couldn't stop, because I knew he would beat my ass. I ran into my aunt's house, ran into her arms, and held her tight, because I was afraid, he would come into the house. She was confused about what was going on, so I confessed that he was the one who had hit my face. Eventually, my aunt and his mom exchanged words.

Later on in life, when I was about twenty-five years old, I went back to Jamaica to visit. I was walking one day, when I heard someone call my name. "Tiny?" I looked at the man, and his face was slightly familiar, although I didn't remember who he was. He said, "It's me,

Dwayne." I pondered for a moment, trying to remember who he was. He then said, "The guy you tried to beat up during the game?" My guard was immediately up. I said, "Oh, Dwayne, I remember you. How have you been?" We eventually talked about what had happened, and I showed him the scar he had left on my face from hitting me with the stone. He shared with me that he had told his children the story, and had taught them how to play Duck-Duck-Goose as well. At that time, Dwayne introduced me to his girlfriend, but he ended up passing away five or six years after that. He had gotten into an altercation with some guys, and they ended up shooting him. He was on the road to success—he ran his own taxi service. I was happy to know that we got to see each other as adults, and he got to see what he did to my face. He was very apologetic, and he was very remorseful, so rest in peace, Dwayne. I don't get that moment of reconciliation with people often.

In Jamaica, I was treated like a foreign child. They would pay special attention to me, and almost everyone would give me special treatment. But after a while, that treatment stopped. I knew that I wanted to go back home to Canada, because I didn't want the Jamaican life anymore, but my family in Canada didn't want me to come back. I would protest and say, "I'm not Jamaican, and I don't want to live like this any longer." So, when I went to school in Jamaica, it was for a short time, because I would always rebel and stand up for myself. I was not going to be talked down to, even as a child. If an adult was trying to boss me around, I would think to myself, *"Who are you talking to?"* I was in Jamaica for a year. Initially, I had gone there for the Christmas holiday.

Eventually, my passport went missing. My dad had gotten deported to Jamaica during that time as well, so he couldn't bring me back to Canada either. I wasn't speaking with my mother, and my grandmother was working in the States at the time. So, what was I even going back home to? I thought for a moment, *"I might as well stay. It's not like I'm being mistreated here. It's not like I don't know the people here."* As a child, it was tradition that I went to Jamaica for Christmas. So, I went to Jamaica periodically, almost every other holiday, so I was familiar with my community. When I asked my aunt why she would not help me to return to Canada, she said, "When you're in Canada, we hear things, you know. You don't have anybody to guide you, and your dad's not doing the best when it comes to parenting. Yes, he provided some things, but we know what your dad's about, so just stay here."

I told her, "You can't make that choice for me." Ultimately, I made the decision that I was unhappy and wanted to leave. I literally asked around, and a lady named Lynn told me where the Canadian Embassy was. My aunt and Lynn weren't talking at the time, and now Lynn has passed away. I went to the Canadian Embassy, because I thought, *"I'm Canadian. I don't need to be here. I want to send myself back home."* That was how I was able to return to Canada. Still, I'm grateful for growing up in Jamaica, because there were tools and things I learned while I was there that I apply to my everyday life, even now.

When I was thirteen years old, my mother had another child, my sister. She was born prematurely; therefore, she was not able to come home to us right away and had to stay at the hospital for a while after her birth. Soon after, my mother got into a car accident, which led to my taking over the care of my brother, Jesus, which I did not mind at all. On weekends, I would bring him to my godmother's house, and he was able to experience *The Cosby Show* lifestyle that I had always told him about. On weekdays, I lived with my father and his girlfriend, although my brother and I were usually home alone.

One day, my brother and I were home with my mother's new boyfriend, Jeff. He asked me a dumb and uncomfortable question: "Do you have a boyfriend?" He probably asked because I was a tomboy to the core. I would wear my hair in one of two ways: either pigtails or a ponytail. On Sundays, my mother would wash my hair, treat it with mayonnaise, and then press it. Later that day, I would go outside to play with a young man named Sheldon, at the park. One Sunday afternoon, as we were playing, he threw sand in my clean hair. I wasn't happy about it, because my mother was hotheaded, and I knew she would beat my ass. That beautiful evening, I fought Sheldon Bailey like a boy, and I fractured his nose on the playground. I was a fighter back then. We all have a bit of crazy in our childhood.

When Jeff asked me if I had a boyfriend, I said, "Of course, I have a boyfriend, but I am not going to tell you who it is." His next question was, "Does he kiss you and stuff?" I looked at him, and then I asked him, "What are you talking about?" I became uncomfortable to the point of cursing the hell out of him. He called my mom and told her

everything that I'd done. She came straight home from the hospital, boiling with anger.

My mother, of course, did not ask me any relevant questions. Straightaway, she shouted, "Why are you trying to break up my relationship?"

As a thirteen-year-old, I quite understood what it felt like to be wrongfully accused. My feelings were hurt, because that truly wasn't the intent of my heart. My response to her was simply, "What are you asking me? Like, are you crazy? Non!"

I thought that would have been the end of it, but incidents like that occurred many other times. Jeff would ask me inappropriate questions and, eventually, he started trying to hold one of my hands. The way he held my hand puzzled me. I asked him, "What are you doing?" I took the pen that was on the table, and I stabbed him with it.

He yelled, "I'm going to tell your mom!"

I said, "When you tell her, tell her why you are holding my hand. Choose not to hold my hand and there won't be any problem." I further told him that I was going to tell my dad, and he was very upset about that. Then he put his hand over my mouth and pleaded with me, multiple times, not to tell my dad.

29

Chronicles of Jane: The Jane Print

I never told my dad about the incident. Jeff definitely crossed the line, but he didn't do anything to me sexually. I sensed it was going there, though, so I made sure to stop his foolish antics immediately, before things got out of hand. I never told anyone about it; I kept it between Jeff and me. Not that it was a secret, nor was I protecting him. I just chose not to disclose it. One day, my godmother asked me, "What were you and Jeff arguing about?" I didn't go into details with her, I only revealed that he had asked me questions that were inappropriate, and so I stabbed him with a pen. To my surprise, he hadn't told anyone about what I had done to him. My godmother is so Canadianized that it was disrespectful to her to speak in Jamaican patois. I had to communicate with her in standard English. Oh, how I love her!

For six months, I stayed away from my mother's house because of what I had disclosed, and I stayed with my godmother instead. My godmother was very overprotective of me. Since I was not in my mother's home when my sister was born, I didn't get a chance to hold her. At first, I had a limited opportunity to know her, but as time went by, I got to know her. My mother's instinct probably spoke to her, because she eventually ended her relationship with Jeff. Not too long after my mother's failed relationship with Jeff, she introduced me to a gentleman by the name of Paul, from Jamaica. He was a good-looking, clean-shaved, light-skinned man. However, he had no status in Canada, so he needed his permanent resident papers. Keep in mind that my mother was still legally married to my dad, despite the many men connected to her throughout the years.

Paul was a weird person, just like my mother. He wasn't a drug addict, which was a good thing, but he was broke. He didn't see me on weekdays, only on the weekends. I was considered the weekend child, who had the full responsibility of taking care of my brother and sister. Whenever I got to spend time with them, I would take them outside in the evenings, and we would play together. One evening, Paul was prepping for Sunday dinner—it was either a Friday or a Saturday. I believe this is a Caribbean thing. As he cooked in the kitchen, I sat at the dining table, eating pop tarts. The kitchen was enormous, spacious enough for him to do what needed to be done. Paul turned around, looked me straight in the eyes, and said, "You know, for a little girl, you should be doing more in this house whenever you visit us."

I turned to Paul, looked into his eyes, and said, "You can't give me chores! Who are you? What's your name again?"

He got upset and said, "Well, I'm the man of this house."

My response was, "No! This house is Metro Housing, and the man of this house is my brother. Your name is not on any papers here." I knew this because my grandmother told me many things that were happening with, and to, my mother. I continued to say, "You can't put me out when I leave. This house is a three-bedroom, and it can't turn into a two-bedroom. I don't care if you tell my mother! What is she going to do? Beat me? I'm used to that."

31
Chronicles of Jane: The Jane Print

Paul was infused with so much anger towards me that he picked up the Dutch pot cover and threw it at me. When he did that, I was like, "What!" He had definitely picked up that behaviour from my mother, and he thought he could abuse me the same way she did. As parents, we must be very careful about the way we treat our children in the presence of others, especially our significant others. Well, his thoughts betrayed him. I wasn't taking it. I started to curse him by the tips of my toes. I cursed him out. When my mother arrived home, I was outside doing my own thing. He told her what had happened between us. I knew deep within me what was coming after. The weekend was ending, and I was getting ready to leave soon to go back to my father's house. That is why I cursed him out so badly—I knew that I wouldn't have to stay at my mom's place much longer. My mother, easily deceived by her partner, asked the neighbour to get me, since I was playing outside. I didn't want to go, to be honest, but I was a child, so I went inside to face the music. I'd be going with my dad soon, I reminded myself.

My mother and Jeff's place was at the end of the tunnel of the Metro Housing complex. When I entered the house, I went into the kitchen and opened the window. I had a strategic plan to make sure that when my dad was coming for me, he would hear the raucous sound from the tunnel. Paul explained the altercation we had, defending himself to my mother, and she immediately dragged me to the corner of the wall. She wanted to defend her stupid man. I noticed that Paul had left out that he had thrown the Dutch-pot cover at me, so I brought it up at that

very moment. I said, "He left out the part where he threw the Dutch pot cover at me, and there's a dent in the wall."

She said, "That's what happened?"

I said, "Ask him how that hole got in the wall."

She turned to him and asked, "Did you throw the pot cover at her?" Paul confessed and admitted what he had done to me. My mother let go of me, and they started to fight. I began to cheer for my mother. I never knew I could cheer for my mother like that. It was the best feeling ever. She beat that man, and I said, "Yes!" At the same time, I was confused, because I was usually the victim, and I had never seen her defend me before. She continued to beat him to a pulp. As I was passing Paul, I kicked him, and it felt so good.

My father came to pick me up from my mother's house, and he asked, "What's going on?" He had witnessed my mother and Paul fighting, and had pulled out his gun. Paul started to plead and explain himself. Knowing me and my prideful self, I said, "No! Ha-ha, he threw the Dutch-pot cover to hit me, and he also said I must wash plates! Remember, I don't live here regularly." My dad turned to him and asked him three times, "Did you give my daughter rules?"

He lied at first, because of the sticky situation he was in, and his nose was already bleeding. I entered the conversation again and said, "No, he's lying! He threw the pot cover at me while he was yelling and screaming." By this time, Helen had taught me not to lie, but sometimes I would exaggerate, so I made the story juicier.

My dad then said, "You're in here beating up on her mom?" My mom jumped in and said, "No, he wasn't beating up on me."

He made a decision and said to Paul, "Pack up your stuff; you have to leave." My dad helped him pack his little blue suitcase, and put him right out.

When I came back inside, my mom said, "Oh, you mash up my relationship!"

I said, "I what? I fully admitted that he threw the pot cover at me, and you bust his ass. You watched your husband put him out." My mother decided to beat my ass, but I didn't cry. I just took the beating, and that was that. I found out later that when I was not there, Paul was there. My brother told me that Paul still came over. I guess he feared my being there, and that I would tell my dad. Finally, they broke up and she moved to Mississauga.

My mother had a new boyfriend named Kirk, and, of course, she got pregnant again. I felt the need to be a nurturer; therefore, I helped her look after my brothers and sisters. One day, my mom was on her way

to work, and she had another accident. It was winter, and the building had five steps to get into it, but they didn't salt the steps, so she ended up falling. She fell down the steps and broke her ankle, to the point where the doctors had to put screws in it. She needed help with the children, because she wasn't family-oriented. Therefore, she left me to care for them. The good thing about me was that I was always ready to help. She promised me that she wouldn't hit me as much as before, but I knew within me that that was a lie. I didn't like when she hit me; nonetheless, I'd rather take the beating myself than let my brothers or sisters endure the pain. There was a time when I travelled to the lake behind our buildings to skate. *The Cosby Show* life showed me how to skate, but my brother didn't know how to ice skate. I still brought him to the lake. He had on a green snowsuit. I said to him, "Come on the lake." Lo and behold, he took one step on the lake, and he sat on it. It wasn't a lot of snow, but it was cold. He sat down and played in the snow. While he played, I was on the lake twirling. Suddenly, I heard the ice cracking. All I could say was, "Oh, my God!" So, I told him not to come on the ice. I tried to run back to him, but the ice gave way. All I could do was look up, and I saw my brother running in the snowsuit back to the building. I tried to catch him, because if he got to that building before me, I was going to get a proper beating. But the ice was giving way. By the time I got out of that water, my brother was long gone. You know, when I got home, I got a proper beating.

My mother said to me, "Oh, you want to come here and act like the dead?"

I said, "I nearly died in the lake. Quel est le problème? I'm cold and wet, and you're yelling and screaming and carrying on."

My mother did beat me that day. All she could say was, "Suppose you killed my child?"

"But he wasn't even near the lake, though," was my response.

That was her only concern—her Jesus, my brother. I didn't come back to spend a weekend for a while, and when I did come back, my mother had herself another boyfriend, and he was a street guy. He also knew my dad from the streets, so whenever I came over, he was very polite to me. For instance, he would say to me, "Did you do your homework?" At first, I didn't answer, but when my mom used to yell and hit me, he would say to her, "You can't do that. I don't want anyone, including her dad, to think I'm encouraging this behaviour.

You know how the streets are run."

My mother was very particular about her home. No matter where she lived, she was always clean. I was fourteen years of age when she decided to make the move. I made it my duty to keep the place neat and tidy, especially for the sake of peace, but knowing the person my mother was, nothing I did was ever good enough. As I was cleaning the house one day, her boyfriend said to me, "If you move the figurine, she will notice." It was a nice evening. My mother came home from work, and she saw a fork in the sink that my brother had left there. She

started to curse in Jamaican. She said, "Bumboclot!" I wasn't sure why she was cursing, since I had cleaned up the entire apartment perfectly. Then my brother looked at me and said, "The fork". So, I said, "You didn't wash the fork, really?" Then we both heard her yell, "Kamelah!" She started to curse in Jamaican, again. I went into the kitchen, and I had on my headphones. I was listening to Wu-Tang Clan on my Walkman. She was calling me all types of names, including "bitch," and so in my head, I was calling her names back, not knowing the words were actually coming out of my mouth. She heard me, and when I turned around, I saw her.

I saw her lips moving, but I couldn't hear what she was saying, because the music volume was too high. I watched her as she picked up the brass stand and wacked me across my forehead with it. That's all I remember. When I woke up, I felt really warm. I still have the scar today. She gave me a gash straight across my face. Her boyfriend said to her, "She needs to go to a hospital."

She just called him crazy, saying they would take the other kids away. She didn't want me to go to Helen's, she didn't want me to go to my dad's, and she didn't make me go to school. They just dressed the wound for a short time.

When I ended up going to my godmother's house, she asked, "How did you get that cut on your face?" I told her about the lake story, and

she said, "Okay. Did you go to the doctor?" And I said, "No." So she ended up bringing me to a doctor.

The doctor said, "I don't know who puts Vaseline and iodine on this, but you need stitches." So, I got stitches that same day.

When my dad saw me, he asked, "How did you get that cut?" And I told him the truth. He said, "Why didn't you tell Helen the truth?" I said, "Well, I did tell her the truth about the lake, but I just didn't tell her about the other story, because it was in the same timeframe. I knew what the outcome would be, and I didn't want my brothers and sisters to be taken away from the family and end up in the system. So, I told a half-truth."

My dad went to my mother's house and said, "Enough is enough! She's not coming back here, because the hit you gave her cracked her skull." The X-ray showed that that was the case. So that was it. I was sad, because I wouldn't be seeing my brothers and my sisters, although they sometimes called me. She ended up having a son for that boyfriend, and they moved back to Jane and Finch. I was in high school when she made the decision to relocate there. They moved to the heart of Jane and Finch, close to my high school. I started to see my brothers and sisters regularly, and I saw my mom basically every day in the mall. She would stop to see a friend in the mall after work. Her friend had a restaurant, and I would pass through there with my friend. Sometimes I didn't say hi, and sometimes I did. Unfortunately, by this time, my

father had been deported. I never told anyone. She got word of it, though, and said, "Well, come stay with me." At the time, I was travelling from Newmarket to go to school. It was a long journey back and forth, and it was becoming hectic. So, I took her up on her offer. She was hardly home, so I ended up watching the children. To be honest, the physical abuse stopped, and it was now just verbal abuse. Her primary focus was work and then hanging out with her friends. Then she started travelling a lot. I was home alone with the kids. One of the trips was longer than usual. She left, and then she never came home. She was usually away for a week or two weeks, but now it had been a month. My dad wasn't in the country at the time, as he had gone to the United States.

I was getting the kids ready, dropping them to daycare, and attending school myself. The daycare teacher suspected something wasn't right, and one day decided to follow me home, after I picked up the kids. I thought she was just nosy, but maybe she was just concerned. She knocked on the door, and I opened it for her. She asked, "Where's your mom?"

I said, "She's at work."

She said, "No problem. I'm going to sit here until she returns."

I said, "Okay. Well, do you want a glass of water?"

39
Chronicles of Jane: The Jane Print

I thought to myself, *"What am I going to do?"* Suddenly, I remembered my god-sister. I always thought she was really cool. Even though they lived in Newmarket, she worked in Toronto. So, I went into the bathroom and called her. "I can't find my mom. She's not home, and the teacher is sitting here and she wants to talk to an adult." I explained everything to my god-sister on the phone. She was at work and was able to leave, so she said she'd be there in half-an-hour. When I hung up, I turned to the daycare teacher and said, "Okay, she'll be here in an hour. She's at work." Lo and behold, she came in twenty minutes, only to be met with the teacher's demands to see my mother.

"Her mother is doing a double shift, so I'm here to stay with them." She was working at some office, and she pulled out a badge to show the teacher. They had a short conversation, and then the teacher left. My god-sister didn't know I was home alone regularly with my younger siblings, and she inquired about my mother's whereabouts.

"Ok, what's going on?" elle a demandé.

I had no answer to give. Days later, we found out that my mother was in jail for importing drugs. My godmother and her friend went to bail her out. That was another milestone for me.

When my mother came home, she said, "You actually held out?"

I said, "It was like a month. Where were you for a month? You left me with your three children to deal with, and I'm a child. I have things to do. I don't have time for this. Even the teacher followed me home."

I knew that she had money in her room whenever she went away, but I didn't want to touch it. My dad's girlfriend at the time gave me lunch money anyway, so that's what we were surviving off of. And anytime my mother travelled, she would do a proper grocery shopping first, so there were groceries still in the house. I would cook for the kids and make sure they were fed.

When she came out of prison, she reasoned with me. She told me, "Well, I don't want you to look down on me, but this is something I've been doing for years." She took the time to explain it to me. The conversation was over an hour long, and it was very detailed. It was as if she was educating me on the streets. I already knew both my parents were from the streets, but my godmother didn't want me in that type of environment. She said to my mother, "You need to figure out what to do with the kids, and call their father to sort things out, because you have these charges against you, and you could get a lot of jail time." Afterwards, my mother began to think about what her next steps would be.

CHAPTER FOUR:

INSTABILITY BEFORE THE FALL

My mother ended up moving to St. Clair West for some time. I guess the police knew her address, because it didn't take her long before she relocated to the heart of Jane and Finch. She changed her addresses frequently, maybe it was because of her street life. On the eve of my birthday, September 16th, my mother asked me if I could watch the kids for her. I agreed to it; however, I expressed to her that I already had big plans with my friends. We were planning on going to the movies, getting something to eat, going downtown, and shopping at the Eaton Centre. I also had a seven o'clock appointment to get my hair done—nothing extravagant, I just wanted my hair to be washed, treated, and pressed. I was going out with my friends, so I had to present myself well, and on top of that, it was in the downtown area where all the upper-class people either lived or went to hang out. Even though my dad wasn't in the country, he still used to pay my hairdresser bill. My father was so well known that he had connections everywhere. He was friends with the owner of a sneakers store in the Jane and Finch Mall. It was a drug-related friendship. Every week, I got a new pair of sneakers, plus I got to do my hair, because my dad would pay them in advance for whatever shoe or style I wanted. Even though I didn't do my hair often, as I was never that girly, I didn't like to comb my hair myself. I couldn't manage all of my hair. Whenever I didn't use my credits at the shoe store or hairdresser, my friends would utilize it. There was a restaurant in the mall, and my dad, or his friends, would pay the owner one hundred dollars a week, so I could go there and get what I wanted.

My mother wasn't the most loving towards me; however, I didn't mind watching the children for her so she could go about her business, as long as she came back on time. That afternoon, I decided to watch the kids from the hallway. I opened the door, and used the telephone book to prop the apartment door open. I never actually went into her apartment. It's not that I was not welcome in the apartment, but I just had my own plan for that day. I instructed them on what to do. I would tell them to go and have a bath, and then they came to the door with the lotion and Vaseline for me to lotion their skin. Afterwards, I helped them with their homework at the door. I stayed on the hallway carpet the whole time. I paged my friend to get them Happy Meals from McDonald's.

It was seven o'clock, and I was still babysitting when I should have been out with my friends. When I saw that it was eight o'clock, I thought to myself, *"The time to hang out with my friends has passed, and my hair is still in a mess."* I said to the kids, "Okay, go into your rooms and lay down. I'm going to stay right here at the door until she comes." The superintendent of the building cleaned at night. He had his mop and vacuum in his hands, ready to work. He kindly asked me to go into the unit so he could do his job. "Damn it," I said to myself. So, I ended up going into the apartment. The telephone book was still holding the door open while he was cleaning. I stood right at the door and, eventually, I got tired of standing. I went back and forth in my mind about whether to get a dining chair to sit on. I knew my mother to the core, and I didn't want her to come and say that I had done anything to her apartment or that her place was dirty. I wanted to avoid doing the little things that triggered her. I wanted her to come home and see her place the same way it was before I got there. The children woke up, and our mother was still not home. I instructed them to stay with me by the door, because I didn't want them to touch anything. I went and threw the garbage from the Happy Meals into the garbage chute, so there were no problems when she came home. The old man was almost finished cleaning, when my mother and her friend came out of the elevator. They had their bags and boxes in their hands. I stood there and watched them struggle as they walked towards the unit. I was ready to leave.

She was mad that her door was open and asked if someone was there. I said to her, "Listen, let me tell you something: I wasn't even in the unit for twenty minutes. I've been in the hallway the whole time."

This woke my brother up, and he confirmed to her, "No, we were inside. She was in the hallway."

My mother asked, "They weren't in the hallway?"

We all said, "No," at the same time. I told them to go back to bed and that I would see them soon.

I said to her, "They ate McDonald's, they bathed, and they did their homework. I'm leaving." I didn't ask her any questions as to why she stayed so long.

She pushed me against the wall and said, "Oh, I have to check the house first."

I laughed and replied, "You can do whatever you want. I'm leaving." The mop was close to her, by the kitchen, and while I was passing, she hit me with it. I grabbed the mop stick from her. "You can't hit me again; I'm not a kid. What are you doing? I just want to leave."

Her friend said, "You know she didn't do anything if she watched the kids from the hallway. She must have a reason why she did that." I said to her friend, "You see how she's behaving? This is the reason I did that."

45
Chronicles of Jane: The Jane Print

She pushed back to get the mop stick away from me, and I let it go. Oh, she created a scene. She was claiming that I hit her with the mop stick, but her friend saw exactly what had taken place, and knew that what my mother uttered wasn't the truth. She tried to hit me one more time, as I made my way to the door. Then she barricaded the door and called the police. I did not move until they got there. She told the police that I hit her. So, I said, "Could you call my godmother? I have no clue what she's talking about. Could you please just call this number, and speak with her?"

The officer said with authority, "Well, the parent is saying that her child is abusing her. What do you want us to believe?" What he said confirmed what I already knew—he didn't believe me. I said, "I don't even live here."

The officer asked me, "What are you doing here?"

"Oh my gosh, she asked me to babysit the kids. I babysat the kids from the hallway." The officer was confused. He asked, "Why would you do that?"

I explained that she was very particular about the way her house was kept. Then I said, "I don't have the time for this. Can I just go, immediately?"

My mother put on a piece of *Days of Our Lives* acting, as if she was this concerned parent, and implied that something might be wrong with me. Her friend had left when she called the police. The police officer asked if any witnesses were there. I told them that the kids could tell them. My brother came and wanted to speak up. However, my mother shoved him away and directed him into the room. They called my brother again, and he said to the officer, pointing, "I sat right there and ate my McDonald's, and she helped us with some colouring and stuff."

The police asked him what happened after, but he didn't have an answer to that.

They went aside and had a conversation, but by the way the officer looked at me, I knew he sided with her and believed her over me. I was later transported to Covenant House. Covenant House is a youth shelter. I didn't know Helen's number by heart, and they took my pager and my phone book away. I looked it up in the general phone book, but it was not listed. Afterwards, I remembered the bakery that was close to where my godmother lived. The baker and Helen were close friends. I looked up the bakery's number, got in touch with that specific baker, and filled her in on what was taking place. My godmother and my father's girlfriend came to the youth shelter, and his girlfriend signed for me to be released. I was out of there in less than a week. That was the good part; the sad part was I turned sixteen in custody. I don't know how they got word that I was there, but I was

called to the office, and I saw my dad's girlfriend and Helen. My dad's girlfriend signed me out, not my godmother. I don't know why, and I did not ask. The incident with my mother happened around ten o'clock, and by the time I got to the station, it was after midnight. After I got out of custody, my godmother, my dad's girlfriend, and I went to get something to eat at Harvey's. While at Harvey's, Helen said, "Well, your mom was wrong for what she did. I know you did not do the things she said. However, your money is on its way."

I was like, "Huh? Quoi?" I didn't remember anything about any money. A few minutes later, it all made sense. It brought me back to the time I stayed with my aunt in New York when I was younger. She had entered me in a baby pageant contest. However, I wasn't able to access the prize money until I was sixteen.

My mother remembered that, and she thought my saying that I had things to do meant that I was going to spend all the money on my friends and buy foolishness. So, knowing I was going to get the money the next day, she intentionally called the police to prevent that from happening. I didn't even remember anything about the money. It was far from my mind, because I never lacked anything. My stepmother at the time had three kids for my dad. She used to take care of me. She bought me nice clothes, brought me to get my hair done, and provided food for me to eat. She had a lot of friends from the streets, so whenever I got clothes from her, it was usually a lot. And I was allowed to wear her clothes, even though I had my own. So,

I didn't need that

money. I never dwelt on it. Once I left Covenant House, I stopped talking to my mother. What she had done didn't make sense to me. But I never let that get in my way, because it had already happened, and there was absolutely nothing I could do about it.

My mother and I couldn't get along, no matter how hard I tried to please her. I was overjoyed when I got news that my dad was coming back to Canada. As I mentioned before, he had gotten deported by the police because of the life he was living. This occurred numerous times. I thought my dad would have never stepped foot on these grounds again, but he did. As soon as he arrived, he rented us an apartment at Jane and Wilson. It was a little building—three stories, no elevator. I was still in high school at the time. I used to go to his baby mother's house close by; he had also rented an apartment over there for her. It so happened that her three kids ended up staying with us for a while, because she was caught by the police and was imprisoned. So, I had to take on the role of their mother and care for them. Upon her release from prison, she came to live with my dad, me, and her kids, but for some reason, we didn't get along. I can recall the physical fight we had over my en suite. Her plan was to take over my bedroom, because it was big and had an en suite. My anger towards her consumed me, and I said to her, without fear, "This is my room!"

She replied, "Oh, but you are a child."

I responded, "I cannot live here any longer. I have had enough of you! You do not appreciate the fact that I have watched and cared for your children for six months while you were behind bars." My dad overheard what was transpiring between us, and yes, my dad sided with me. After all, I am his first child, whom he loves dearly. He said to her, "You know what? She's been taking care of the kids. I'm in the streets, and I don't have time for that. She's been here with the kids most of the time."

You would think that my dad had learned his lessons by now, but he hadn't. He was still on the streets, doing his transactions. This woman my dad was with didn't want me to have company over. She created a lot of rules that I wasn't used to. Deep within me, my instinct said, *"I can no longer live here."* I needed my own space and peace and quiet. So, I said, "You know what? Here's what is going to happen. You guys can keep this apartment, and I'll move back to the old apartment."

He said, "Okay, but that's not going to happen today."

I said, "Well, I will go to my godmother." My godmother's house was always open to me, and I had my own room.

The words that I spoke pierced my father's heart. He wasn't going to lose his daughter over someone who disliked her, in this case his baby mother. As time went by, it was just me and my dad once more in the apartment, and he kept running the streets and living his life. We hardly

had time for each other; he was too busy doing his thing. I mostly heard his voice when he called or came in late.

You may ask, "So where is your mother in all of this?" The truth is, there still wasn't any form of communication between us. However, my siblings weighed heavily on my mind. I missed seeing them and getting them sneakers ever so often, because I had the sneaker connection. If I did get my brothers and sisters sneakers, I would drop it off at their daycare for them. That was the only way to see them. My dad eventually got the apartment back for us. It was empty at the time, but my dad always got groceries.

I remember coming in from basketball one day to find no dinner, no call, no lunch money. It was the same thing the next day and the day after that. That was not like my dad at all. He never came home. A week later, he passed a message with somebody, saying he was in jail. I didn't know what I was going to do. I had this empty apartment, and all I had was clothes. Since his baby mother and I had argued, she stopped giving me clothes. One thing about me is that I never gave up on school. So, my bed for the time was my clothes. I got up every morning, brushed my teeth, washed my face, and got ready. The only thing I ate was boiled eggs, macaroni and cheese, and noodles. The groceries ran out, and my dad's friends that were normally there for me were either disappearing for a period, dead, deported, or in jail. I could've gone back to my godmother's house, but I did not want her to question me about my dad. He had one or two friends. They used to check up on me, but they thought I was at the other apartment. They didn't know that I had moved. I saw one of them one time at the mall, and he gave me two hundred dollars. I used the two hundred dollars to get some groceries and buy stuff for myself. I didn't want to feel left out when I was out with my friends.

I had a best friend named Tyson. She lived at Jane and Finch, and I liked to go to her house a lot. Sometimes I would even sleepover on the weekends, because I didn't want her mom to ask me about my dad. Everybody knew my mom and I didn't get along, so they didn't ask me about her much. I would go by Tyson's house after school, and by seven o'clock I would go home. Little did they know that I was going home to an empty apartment. I had no TV, and there was no internet in those days, so it was just me, my thoughts, my clothes, and my homework. That lasted for two months. During that time, a white man would knock on the door, but I never answered it. He came back religiously, sometimes two times a day. And one day he said, "Well, I know somebody is here," and he pushed a Leon's Furniture card under the door. It said, "Call me." I never did. I also didn't turn it over until that weekend when I was cleaning up. It was a Leon's card. I guess it was one of my dad's clients. Then I remembered seeing a letter from Leon's. The man wrote me a long note, but I never paid attention to flyers that people pushed under the door; I would just push them to the side or throw them away. One day, the note said, "Well, I know your dad is not here, and I had made a promise to him.

I was here to furnish the apartment, but you refused to open the door. So please give

me a time. I can drop it off." After that, I started to open up all the other letters. He'd been writing to me and wanting to bring the furniture for about a month.

I took the bus and went to the store. I gave the card to a lady at the front desk. She said, "Well, he's not in today. He will be here tomorrow."

I said, "Okay, could you have him call me?" I gave her my phone number, and he ended up calling me the next morning.

He said, "Tiny,"—only somebody who knew my dad would call me Tiny, because, at the time, I had outgrown that name.

I said, "Yes."

He said, "You got my letter, finally. Est-ce que ça va?"

I said, "Yes."
"Oh, can I stop by today and give you some money?" Il a

demandé. I said, "I'm fine."

He said, "Okay, well, I'm going to stop by on Wednesday and deliver some of the furniture. What size bed do you want?"

Chronicles of Jane: The Jane Print

At the time, I didn't know how to size a bed, so I just said, "A bed."
"Do you want a big bed?"

I remembered that my mom always had a big bed, and I was afraid of it, because it was so big. I said, "No, I don't like the big beds." I didn't know it was called a king-sized bed at the time.

"Okay then, I can get you a queen."

I said, "I am a queen, so that's what I deserve."

Lo and behold, he did come. He brought me a lovely black leather reclining sofa, carpet, a coffee table, end tables, a TV, a dining table, and a microwave stand. He also brought me a full bedroom set. It couldn't even fit in the room. I ended up putting one of the night stands by the dining table. I was eternally grateful to God for providing. Nobody knew what I was going through at the time, because I acted normal. God came through for me. I had a fully furnished apartment. I danced that evening. Yes, I danced. I danced. I danced until I fell asleep. But funny enough, I never slept on the bed. I still slept on the floor, for a few days; there was now a carpet, though. A week or two later, I started to sleep on the sofa, and then I began to sleep on the bed. However, I was still home alone, and somewhat low on money.

CHAPTER FIVE:

THE ENGINEERS

A brand-new school year was about to begin. My birthday was around the corner, and I was turning seventeen years of age. My dad had returned, and he was so proud of me for managing things on my own. He said, "I'm so proud of you. You kept yourself out of trouble." Then he handed me some money.

I responded, "If you ever knew how many days I would hate coming here."

"So what time is your friend coming?" Il a demandé.

"No, no one comes here. I was here by myself the whole time. I went to school and still obtained good grades, and I was home by eight o'clock on weekdays. The furniture arrived late, because I did not open the door to your friend." It was just the way of the streets. I wouldn't open the door to this white man that I didn't know, not at my primary location.

We eventually moved in with his girlfriend, and that apartment became a base for his friends. A few months passed, and he ended up being wanted again by the police. I said to myself, *"This is getting out of hand now."*

The police would harass me, and I didn't want to experience that again. My godmother brought me to a place downtown to take off his last name, and I got my mother's maiden name, Blair. Helen thought that the harassment would slow down or stop, but the police knew who I was. They would come to my high school and my hang-out places, when they couldn't find my dad. It became a bit much after a while, so I started to build resentment towards my dad, again. I didn't want my dad's troubles. His troubles were my troubles, but I was only just his child; I was not his actions. Moreover, I'm a girl. Their main problem was that I knew more than I would tell them. I told them absolutely nothing, in fact. Whenever they questioned me about his whereabouts, I would tell them, "When you find him, you let me know. I haven't seen him for years, or months, and I want the child support he owes my mother." That was my line that I said to them every time.

I used to be out with my dad in the streets at nights with his friends. I would help the group rob people. While being raised by my godmother, I was in a Girl Guides group. I hardly went door-to-door selling cookies. My dad and his friends would just buy the boxes. I utilized my Girl Guides uniform to knock on people's doors and say that I'm lost. Someone would open the door, and the group would rob them. That was my job at night. I learned how to drive by participating in this activity, which started at the age of fourteen. We didn't do it every night, but at least once a week. If not once a week, then my dad would bring me on his home invasions every other week. His friends would ask if I could come with them, wearing the Girls Guide uniform, but the look I used to give them never needed an answer.

I had a gold chain with two solid gold dice, and the numbers were diamonds. I wore that chain daily, to the point where my friend called me Jax. I would walk through the mall after school, wearing the chain and dressed like a tomboy. I always had on a tracksuit, either Adidas, Nike, Phat Farm, or Puma. I used to roll up one pant leg, like a little boy, and I always had on the latest sneakers. By this time, I had stopped doing pigtails, because pigtails were too childish. I only wore my hair to the side or the back in a ponytail. One particular day, I had on the Eagles jacket, a black and green Nike tracksuit, and a pair of Scottie Pippen Nikes. Back in the day, every week, girls would meet up with fights. I only lost two fights in my life. I could fight. I was also a mouthpiece, and because I could speak Jamaican more than the regular Canadian, I could curse you out and make you want to fight me. I tore down that mall regularly, and ate at McDonald's repeatedly. I think I was banned from the mall every week, and I was still back, but the people knew my dad, so they couldn't really ban me.

In those days, the big stores in the mall were Woolco and BiWay. *One day, as I was* coming around the corner, where the restaurant was, my mom was there drinking soup on the right side of the restaurant. I stopped and asked the chef, "What's on the menu?" from the left side of the restaurant. He gave me a list of dishes, and I picked fried chicken, rice and peas, salad, and gravy on the side. I went to a sneaker store to see what was new, while I waited on my food. As I entered, he said, "I've got new stuff. You're going to love it," and he pinched my cheeks. He showed me six pairs, and I wanted all six. "I'll pick it up Friday," I said.

"Oh, Bella," he said, "I know. They will be waiting for you."

My best friend, Tyson, and I used to dress the same. I would get my sneakers for free, and she got hers for half price. A few times, I got her free ones. I was so excited to let her know about the new sneakers he had shown me. While walking back into the restaurant, I was thinking about which tracksuit I was going to buy. There was an upcoming rap battle talent show in two weeks, and a few of my friends were entering.

The chef passed me my food, and I thanked him. A strong gentleman was sitting there, staring at me. I could see him from the corner of my eye, and I could most definitely feel him staring at me. I ordered patties from the other side of the restaurant. *At that other part, there were three or four benches, where you could sit and dine in at the counter*— that's where my mom was sitting down. I said, "Hello."

She said, "Afternoon, Miss," in return.

While the man was sitting on the corner, I could see him from my right.

"Hey, little girl, where you get that chain from?"

I didn't answer him. He asked again, but this time his voice got a bit louder. He turned his head to the corner, so we were looking at each other. "Hey, you mi ah talk to, you nuh hear mi? Where you get that chain from? Answer me."

I looked him straight in his tough face and said, "You can't ask me that. Who are you? You're rude and bright!" By this time, my mom put down her soup cup so hard I could hear it.

The man proceeded to get up, and he draped me up and slapped me in the face, and then he broke the chain from around my neck. I looked in his face, and I remembered him. I just did not know from where. I was more focused on the slap I had just received. I have sensitive skin, so I could feel his handprint on my face.

Goldy jumped up and threw the remainder of the soup at him. My mom, my friend that was passing by at the time, and I fought the man in the mall. We fought him to the point where he was asking us to stop. The chef tried to part the fight, but that did not work. I don't know who told my dad's friends, but they ended up coming to the mall. There was a door close to where we were. They came full force and pulled him out through the side door.

There was a huge excitement in the Jane and Finch mall, even the police ended up coming by this time, and we ended up leaving. When my dad saw my face, he was so upset. My mom called my dad and said, "You have her wearing the stuff you take from people. This could have been worse, and suppose I wasn't there?" They went at it for a while. My dad asked her if she was hurt and if she was okay, over and over. He said "Sorry," multiple times. The man was big, though, like the Incredible Hulk, and he had slapped me back into 1982. Even later that evening my ears were still ringing. My dad went to see Godly, to make sure she was okay, and I went along for the ride and to get food. I could hear my mom saying, "You can't have her outside doing things. She's a girl; she's not a little boy. You cannot have her outside doing certain things. I didn't do the best job. I brought her into this world, and I'm not going to let your lifestyle take her out. She's not with me, but you're not doing any better. You should be proud she's not like us. She doesn't even smoke." She was right, and she was calm. I don't drink to this day. I have never smoked, and I have never touched my dad or my mom's weed.

She sat down and told him, "I can't give her what you and Helen give her, because she has everything." I could tell she felt bad.

My mom never physically gave me money. My mom used to buy me one or two things, but she didn't need to, because, as I said, my dad's baby mother took care of me, so I always had clothes. My aunts in New York used to send me stuff, and my grandmother used to buy me clothes. But I couldn't wear tight clothes, even though I used to wear jogging suits. She didn't like that when I went to Helen's, I had to wear blouses, button-up shirts, cardigans, jeans, and stuff. So, I always had two styles of dressing, because I lived two different lives. right?

"You can't turn her into something that you know to be wrong," my mom said. Godly wasn't the first person to tell him that; his baby mother and Helen told him as well. My mother was upset with my dad after that situation, and she went on and on. "You can't have her up and down at the base, because she's hearing what's going on. You can't have her as the getaway driver." To this day, I drive with two feet— one foot on the brake and one on the gas. That's how I learned to drive. My mom was schooling him and saying, "You can't have Kamelah out here doing your dirty work. People know her, and she goes places on her own. She's popular, you're famous, and I'm popular. Look what just happened. It could have been worse; not because she's your child doesn't mean she's untouchable. She's a girl. You have to try to raise her as a girl. Stop treating her like she's your son." She went to pick up the phone to call Helen, and the three of them got into an argument.

"Well, that was your job. You're supposed to raise her as a daughter. And, you know, you didn't do that. This is all I know— the streets," my dad said.

It was unbelievable to hear Goldy spitting facts while I was in the kitchen, still eating slowly and thinking, *"Who told her so much stuff, in such great detail?"*

My dad did put us in the streets, but he made sure at nighttime that we still read our Bible, and then he would let me jump on the bed. I didn't know what it meant until I got older, and he taught me that my body and mind need exercise before I fall asleep. We used to read the Bible first; wherever it dropped open, we just read it together. He then said, "Jump on the bed, Tiny. Jump, jump, jump." As a child, I looked forward to nighttime jumping and reading with my dad. Funny enough, my Uncle Jah-Jan used to let me do the same thing.

My uncle had passed away around this time. He loved me unconditionally. His passing put a damper on my spirit, because when my dad was in and out of the country, if I couldn't find my dad, I could always find my uncle. My Uncle Jah-Jah was a blind man. He wasn't born blind; he became blind one night at a party. Jah-Jah was a Rastafarian, and he was also in the streets. He was the only blind man to rob a bank. A lot of people thought his going blind would stop him from being a real "OG." However, even though he was blind, he was respected. He loved me so much more because we were born on the same day. There was nothing I asked for that I couldn't get from him. My dad never told me "no." I was never wrong with my dad. I have never been with my uncle. With my godmother, I knew how to get things. If I cried, that was it. "Who troubles Tiny?" She never wanted me to be upset when I was in her presence. I think that's how I learned how to be a con artist. I knew how to get around when I wanted something.

At the time of his passing, I was staying with him downtown, on Dupont, the same time as the altercation in the mall. When he heard what happened, he told me about the new world, which is precisely what we're living in today. He didn't use the word "bitcoin," but he explained it. He described the new world for me. He said, "Tiny, I know that we're not the best example, but you have to do better than what we're doing. I don't know if he knew he was going to pass, but that same week, every day I came home, he sat me down and talked to me. "You're not a boy. You're not a girl. You're not a gangster. You cannot be what we are. You need to break the cycle somewhere, and you need to be the one to break the cycle, because your aunts are terrible." Yes, his sisters could curse you out in five minutes. My great grandparents were hardcore. However, my grandmother was very humble. My grandmother Lynnette was very soft-spoken. She was a very serious business woman, noted in her community, and she loved to travel. Whenever I was in Jamaica, we would sit and have conversations about absolutely nothing. She allowed me to dress girly all the time, because she hated to see me in jeans. When I was home, she made it a point of duty to call me every Sunday after church. Sometimes we just sat there and said nothing. I would ask her, "Are you falling asleep?" And she would say, "No," even though I could hear her snoring. She would feel me and what's going on in the community, and she would let me know that she was travelling out to the country or going up to the big house, where my aunt resided. She always asked me when I was coming back. My grandfather was a gangster. I didn't meet my grandfather, but I had visions of him. When I would share my dreams, they would say, "That's your grandfather."

Even though my dad and Uncle Jah-Jah were doing bad things on the streets, we used to go to church each Sunday, an Orthodox church. I never understood it, because the men stood on one side and the women on the other. You had to take off your shoes and wrap your hair, and they did not speak English most of the time, so I couldn't understand it. My uncle used to explain stuff to me during the two weeks, every day when I came in. My uncle made sure he was home after school, and he used to cook. The food was delicious, even though he was a vegetarian. He said, "Tiny, you're brilliant. You're going to school and getting good marks. Please finish school. Sometimes you have to tell your dad 'no;' don't just agree with what he asks of you. I know that you're trying to be obedient, but don't be disobedient to your path." I didn't understand at that moment, but when he passed, everything he said to me in that two-week period came to light, and at that time, I also found out that I was pregnant.

Uncle Jah-Jah was a tall, heavy-set man, and he was wise. He spoke in quotes. It was never a conversation; it was always wisdom, quotes from the Bible, and quotes from history, but I knew he had an angry side that he never showed to me. I only heard of it. The day of his passing, he got sick. He was in the hospital, and even though he was blind, he was very racist. He was a true Rastafarian, so he still carried that burden of slavery. He took that burden with him. He was talking about Malcolm x and, again, wisdom stuff in the hospital. They ended up calling me at school, because he wouldn't listen. He listened to me, even though I was the little one. He looked at me, and I said to him that day, "What is it that you don't want her to do?"

"This white bitch! She's yelling at me, and she doesn't want me to talk. They're drugging me, and they don't want me to talk." He was speaking wisdom, Bible verses, and slavery stories to them, and they didn't want to hear that. So, my Uncle Jah-Jah passed away from an overdose, because they ended up putting too many drugs in his body. Because of what he said to me in his passing, I knew that I had to change the mindset that I had, or at least try to.

When he would speak, I would listen and say, "You're talking gibberish." But I'm thankful for it, because I've lived to see every gibberish thing come to pass, literally. I knew of the technology that was coming. I knew that there would be no money. I knew that a lot of ungodly things were coming. I knew people would stop being loving. I knew a lot, because my uncle would sit me down and tell me what was coming. "This is what you need to do. You need to prepare yourself," he said. He knew whenever I brought friends over, because he explained that when you lose one sense, another sense gets stronger. He would say, "I know you had a bad day. Smile, Tiny, or sing a song or remix a song, just to make me laugh." He was a very wise man, who would go above and beyond for me, even though he had two children of his own.

CHAPTER SIX:

WISDOM BUILDS A HOUSE

Uncle Jah-Jah was older than my dad. My dad was the youngest. Uncle was a family-oriented man with two children and a wife. He was a graduate of Architectural Drafting and Business Finance from Jamaica. He came to Canada in the late 1970s. He liked to cook, and he also liked to hang out in the community, preferably in a group setting, where he would be able to teach words of wisdom to the street from the Bible. He religiously sang Psalm 91 all the time, with his rhythm, just so people would remember it.

He became blind because of an incident at a club he attended with my parents and a handful of friends. They were all well-dressed when they participated in this party, wearing three-piece suits, furs, and Kangol hats. Somebody at the event had an issue with a group that was in attendance, and a shooting occurred in less than an hour. There were rounds of gunplay, but nobody passed away. However, a lot of people got injured. During the shooting, a large number of beer bottles

shattered, and a piece of glass got into my uncle's eye, which blinded him. He was also shot in his shoulder, and this incident took a toll on him, resulting in his not being able to perform his duties as an architect. In turn, it affected his finances, and his life as a whole. Although he lost his sight, he could still help others in his field of work. However, he was no longer wanted, so all he could do was go back to a life of crime. Even though he was crying "Peace" to a few, he went back to that life, because people looked up to him. He was a father figure in the streets. He was well respected. My uncle also didn't want anything to happen to his brother, which was another reason why he chose to involve himself. He would say, "I'd rather be with you than without you."

My uncle's disabilities did not stop him from doing anything. He would do a robbery or two just to maintain his reputation. My uncle and father had a close bond. When they both came around, the combination was strong. During that time, a lot of my dad's friends were moving to Canada from Jamaica, so my uncle started to detach himself from my dad. His mindset was, "You're not alone, and I would rather be wise than be a man who is just known for a crime."

He would sit me down to speak with me, and he would say, "Tiny, now I know you see what's going on. You cannot teach the next generation what you don't see. I'm letting you know to use the knowledge that I have taken from the streets and apply it to Wall Street. What they teach you in school is what they want you to know. I'm teaching you what you need to know."

As I got older, and as the world changed, these remained lessons that I can pass on to my children, nieces, nephews, friends, and family members. I can also apply the old wisdom to this new world. His passing made me sad, but more so frustrated, because I wanted more knowledge. There were so many puzzles that were not complete, quotes and stories that were not complete, because my next daily lesson did not come. However, I got the answers and learned so much from his funeral. The bishop and others spoke highly of him. When people spoke, and they gave their stories, they said things that he had never told me before. It was as though he was speaking through them to connect with me. There were over twenty people that spoke at my uncle's funeral. The funeral was so powerful that we told the funeral director to give us more time. The director turned and said, "Wow, this was an amazing man." He was also gaining knowledge as everybody else was. They weren't sad. It was lesson after lesson about things that he had said to them, either in passing or while hanging out. I got the answers to the puzzle from the funeral. I was truly grateful. My uncle also taught me how to solve problems. Even when he helped me with my homework, he used to sing it to me in a lullaby. For example, he would sing, "Mary had a little lamb." His singing of the answers was a mechanism for me to remember. Now I know that even when the work gets hard and frustration kicks in, I should try to make it fun by

singing a song and being glad in it. These are things that he instilled in me as a child, as part of the playground.

He would also say, "Consider your friends. You should be able to tell a true friend how you feel, and walk away. But, of course, some people you call friends may just consider you an associate and will want it to get physical. Use your words and be loud. Let your voice be powerful. Don't fight with your words. Say what's on your mind." I explained to him that sometimes my words got me in trouble and made people want to hit me. I probably told them about their mother and auntie, or facts about themselves and their families, which led to a fight because of my words. I did not have to hit you; I could uppercut you with my words, and I could send you to bed with words. I had absolutely no filter. Overall, Jah-Jah spoiled me. The only time I've heard my dad and my uncle argue was about me. When my dad said "no," or put something off to another day, my uncle would say, "No, she's doing it today. Just let her do it today. Tomorrow's not guaranteed to anybody." The battle between them was very dramatic, because my uncle was older, and he was a lot chubbier than my dad. So, it was a battle of wisdom. I was also taught by him to question everything. There was no such thing as a wrong question. Their answers would be different, with great wisdom in both answers. When I was around both of them at the same time, my dad looked up to him, and sometimes when I asked my dad a question, he would direct the question to my uncle. So, both of us were learning.

70
Chronicles of Jane: The Jane Print

After the passing of my uncle, my dad shut down. Oftentimes, he would just randomly ask what I missed most about Jah-Jah. I told him what I missed. He said he missed the same things. I've never seen my dad cry until that day. And I've never seen my dad silent. My dad was silent for a whole month. I would say even more. Even when someone spoke to him, he would just give a yes or no answer. There was no music. There was no talking. But he was very comforting. I believe that my uncle's passing brought my dad back to a humbling place, because I noticed that after my uncle's passing, he didn't go right back to the streets. He kind of took more to his family than the streets. I believe he took heed to his brother's advice to be there for his children daily. My uncle told him, "Your friends are here. If something needs to be done in the streets, you have enough friends." And that's what my dad did—his friends were doing more than what he did. I didn't understand what people knew about my dad, because I never saw that side of him. I knew that they were doing stuff, but my dad was a different person at home, even in my high school years. My dad made my breakfast. My dad made sure he was there, to the point where he was picking me up from high school. Every day, while driving home from school, he used to ask, "What do you want to have when you get in? Cabbage sandwich, corned beef sandwich, or egg sandwich?"—Uncle Jah-Jah used to ask the same question about dinner. And even if he went out, he was back in the morning. After some time, he admitted to me that he had learned from my uncle that when your children are eating, you should be in their presence. While they are eating, you should feed their mind as well. You should sit with someone while you're eating, so you

can also have a conversation to nourish your mind. I then realized that these were the same principles at my godmother's house—we had to eat together. Family was very important to Jah-Jah, and that's why he always wanted to be with my dad; he didn't want him to be alone. Growing up in a community in Jamaica, everyone was like brothers. So being around his friends was also important to my dad. Their troubles became his troubles, and it was hard to let go of the streets.

I then turned into the nurturer for my dad. "Oh, are you okay? How was your day?" And even though I only got short answers, I was okay with it. I started to cook. I used to. I was never allowed to be in the kitchen, but my homework table was in front of the kitchen door, so I would always be looking in. *The first time I stepped into the kitchen, I was hesitant. However, I was able to replicate my dad's meals.* He was shocked and impressed. He gave me a thumbs up with a smile, and even asked for seconds. I had to be there to make sure he had something to eat, because he was not the same person. At one point, my dad ended up sleeping in my room. on the floor. I asked him why, once or twice, and then I just stopped asking. Then, one day, he just stopped. My uncle's passing and my dad's silence led me to be independent, and it led me to take on roles and gain tools that I still use today, because if not for my uncle passing, I probably wouldn't know how to cook. I love Uncle Jah-Jah, and I miss him dearly.

www.ingramcontent.com/pod-product-compliance
Lightning Source LLC
Chambersburg PA
CBHW070335120526
44590CB00017B/2888